Echoes
Neo-Victorian Poetry

by

JaniceT

## Acknowledgments

It is with immeasurable appreciation that I thank my husband and my daughter for their steadfast encouragement and abundant support. Because of them, I am finally bringing these poems to print. Some of these works were written years ago. Some have won awards, others are included in anthologies, but I credit this book entirely to my family. Thank you, Emily, for editing and formatting this book. Thank you, Stanley, for editing these poems, and for inspiring me along the way. Without you two, this book would never be.

## - Index -

# Train of Thought

Embarking on a train of thought
The wheels at first turn slowly
As fuel begins to heat within
The grate until it wholly
Consumes contained convulsing flames
That lick upon the belly
Where water bubbles into mist,
Then steam, through pipes upwelling
To boiler's blaze the engine strains
From jostles and jerks to rolling
And every frame beyond my brain
Are blobs, then streaks, then only
Soft blurs that swim till I begin
To sense a coming peace
As fuel is spent, and fires relent
And vapors all but cease.
I latch the boiler gate and let
It coast into the station
And rest my cooling mind awhile
Awaiting inspiration.

# 1739

'Neath dense, black clouds
Pounding rain on the the ocean
Screaming ice winds
Shoved a ship side to side,
Waters relentlessly
Lurching and rising
And not one place in that
Place to hide.
Plumes of foam bursting
High over the vessel,
Desperate waves grappling
Forward and aft.
All of the thirty six
Men would have perished
All of them, save for but for
One slender craft.
Every man pitched himself
After the dinghy,
Some were but hurled out
Beyond to the sea.
The violence of weather
Exploded around them,
And many a hard gripping
Hand was forced free.
Twenty, the bodies
Blown in all directions,
Four holding fast to the
Ship as she sank.
Twelve then were left to
The jettisoned lifeboat,
And evenly deeply of

*JaniceT*

Deluge it drank.
Those yet uninjured
Began to bail water
While all of the others
In chorus did  moan
Over the thundering,
Billowing ocean
'Till every sound merged
Into one eerie drone.
No vital provisions were
There in the lifeboat,
No warm woolen blankets
To stave off the cold.
For this they had beaten
The rest of their shipmates;
Their own cursed lives to
This misery sown.
Expelled into thrashing,
Vehement, black ocean
Dying men waited
For help would arrive,
And wondered if they should have
Drowned with their crewmates
Or tried, as they had all
Their lives, to survive.

*Echoes*

# Elm Street

Elm Street, now devoid of elms,
Lies naked in the sun
For trees were merely idle things
And mattered to no one.
Ah, lush, green lawns of chamomile
Which so perfumed the air
Now lie 'neath asphalt painted green
And plastic flowers bear.

Birch Street, now devoid of birch,
Lies naked in the sun.
Transition to this modern state
The pride of everyone.
Where once migrating birds would rest
Upon a branch to sing
Now thrive stark rows of wired poles
And droned jackhammering.

Oak Street, now devoid of oak,
Lies naked in the sun
Where people of a common breed,
Quite commonly as one,
Have killed true creativity,
And life, and missed it none
Wherever streets devoid of trees
Lie naked in the sun.

# Johnny's Tavern

Hushed, a slumber, redwood treetops
'Neath a bloated, midnight moon
Autumn breezes ever blowing
Leaves upon a slanted roof.

Nestled deep within the forest
Johnny's Tavern lights are low.
Set to match the cozy quiet
Windows cast an amber glow.

Through the yawning, wooden portal
Into realms of warmth and cheer
Venture the nocturnal patrons
Seeking frosted mugs of beer.

Golden, foaming draft courses each
Throat 'till every fiber sings
Bittersweet sensations as the
Froth melts to a thin, white ring.

Thousand tiny bubbles rising
Up to burst the remnant foam.
Staring deeply into vessels
Each man sees within is home.

Down, down through infinite chamber
'Till the glass, and all, recede.
Captivating, smooth enchantment,
All that there need ever be.

# Twist

A slender man ignores the damp,
That permeates an upper room,
With not but an old oil lamp
To keep at bay the London gloom.

His fixed intent and form are bent
Upon the timepiece in his hand.
Small tools he plies to this device
With more than skill at his command.

Soon comes a sigh to signify
That his repairs are now complete
He notes the face but not the time
And takes another sip of tea.

# Down The Narrow Ghetto Streets

Down the narrow ghetto streets
Of noise and cobblestone
You found me lying at your feet,
My form reduced to bone,
And lifting me most gingerly
You recognized my frame
Though strings and gilded brass were gone
And only wood remained.

Down the narrow ghetto streets
You carried your new prize
Which all abusive handling
Could not from you disguise.
And reaching home you clothed my bone
In little leaves of brass,
Restrung my strings and tuned and honed;
All skill did you surpass.

Down the narrow ghetto streets
Dismantled hand by hand
I lay at last before the feet
Of such a tender man
Who saw in me my finer strings
And thus rebuilt this harp,
So, ever shall I play for you
The motifs of my heart.

*Echoes*

*JaniceT*

# The Vigil

There is an old man named Tim O'Shea
Who sits on a bench in the park.
His daily task – feeding birds all day
On bits of bread until dark.
Oft in his youth he would come to laugh
At old men who sat on the bench.
Yet, now he just smiles through his bountiful years
At young men who pass him and grin.
How well he remembers those elderly men
And the kindness in their smile,
And now he knows that as he had laughed
He'd been laughed at all the while.

# Tavern Lass

Beneath her bodice gleaming white
There dwells a heart of anthracite
Yet, transient sailors do delight
The challenge of her glances.

Across the candle-lit café
Her threatening whispers, "keep away,"
Are ever daily disobeyed,
Her eyes expelling lances.

Each man sits down to banter words
While effortlessly these she spurns.
A tattered ego swiftly turns,
She smiles, the next advances.

And every night, the gaming done,
She sees herself the losing one
Entangled in the web she's spun
That's strangling her chances.

# Emery

Emery had a nose of stone,
An outgrowth of his weighted mind.
Of alabaster was it honed
Into a feature aquiline.

It's heft was such that Emery
Would counterbalance with his jaw
By upward thrust of chin; thus he
Intended to reduce this flaw.

But, oh, his lips contorted and
His limited perception showed
Only a level, skyward span
And never anything below.

Many men were victimized
And many things they valued, too,
Because poor Emery was blind
To that which was not in his view.

The morning of one winter's day
He walked a promontory ridge.
Poor Emery saw not the way
But fell. It was the last of him.

# Fox

Waiting, as a cat upon
Anticipated prey,
A beach without an ocean
Stretches endlessly away
Surrounded by a vacant,
Pale blue sky
And windless 'neath
Ascending solar eye.
Now, centrally in forest lush,
Oh variegated flower,
The playing ground of little Fox
Moves farther by the hour
From dew-dunked foliations
Densely grown
Toward a desolation
Yet unknown.
Consuming and consumed relentless
Folly through the green
Ere slowly eked elastic time
By increments it seemed
'Till suddenly it snapped
In Fox's face
That fertile soil, by sand,
Had been replaced.
A glance in all directions wrought
A silent, violent scream
When moisture, shade, and all that Fox
Had ever blindly seen
Were sharply and mysteriously gone
As when a dream is ripped
Away at dawn.

*JaniceT*

His sun-stabbed eyes glared painfully
From dune to naked dune
Enveloped in the acrid, arid,
Swollen heat of noon.
The desert did
A little game intend
So neither wound nor
Movement would it lend.

By night, the sand assumed a bluish
Whiteness to it's role
Where little Fox lay shivering
On open landscapes cold
And pondered on
A method of release.
'Twas all that bought his
Lonely body peace.
A bloated silver moon stared down
With blank, untempered face
Adorned in deep blue regions
By the stars which patterns traced.
"The stars," thought Fox,
"Which glide across the air.
Perhaps the way back home
Is carried there."
Thus, up he rose on quivering limbs,
Up from the cold, hard bed,
Then out across all landlessness
Where ere the ceiling led.
A brandied warmth
Throughout his body grew
And strength and hope-spun
Daring did renew,
For whether 'twas a pathway home

*Echoes*

Or measures meant to stray
Proved but a minor matter,
Little Fox was on his way
No more to huddle
Through the frozen night
He'd found one means
Of lessening his plight.
Around his muzzle tiny specks
Of midnight moisture clung,
Enough to ease his shrinking throat,
His unabated tongue.
The desert, agitated
And alarmed,
Thought long on methods
To retain or harm.

Where open sky and distant dunes
Are to each other sewn,
A full round, heavy moon was dragged
And quietly deposed.
That very instant
Did the sun arise,
Another witness
From another side.
The glowing warmth of morning crept
Along the graceful dunes
But slowly did the heat begin
To burn before 'twas noon
And little Fox,
perspiring though dry
Felt ever more light's
Needles in his eyes.
Through squinting slits he soon perceived
That every star had gone

*JaniceT*

To sleepy rest from traveling,
But still he ventured on
And tried to keep his straightest
Route in sight,
When suddenly a blur
Off to the right
Brought gasps of free expectancy
To little Fox's heart.
"My home! It must be home!" he cried
And quickly did depart
From everything the stars
To him had shown
Not heeding them
For he was going home.
With all his strength he bounded for
The green, myopic blur
And though he thought he'd reach it soon
This never did occur.
While all day long young
Fox did phantoms chase
The desert dawned a smile
Upon it's face.
It wasn't 'till the sky grew dark
And stars again appeared
That tired Fox could clearly see
What he'd begun to fear;
The blur dissolved
And faded from his sight
And stars were moving
Counter to his plight.

Beneath a starry pathway
Pointing slowly through dark skies
There slowly ambled little Fox,

*Echoes*

With tears still in his eyes.
Then, as the cold increased
So did his pace
And out of anger
Fox resumed his race.
As brute determination bled
From brain to chambered heat
The boundless beach blew silent bugle calls
And armies marched,
So through the quiet
Fox began to hear
A crunching cadence
Beating, beating near.
Upon a dune which overlooked
The desert's broadest range
There little Fox drew to a stop
To view and ascertain
The source of that
Which he now clearly heard
And as he waited, pondering,
It neared.
What first seemed like the sound of twigs
Which to some rhythm snapped
Increased so loudly dense and crisp,
Though little time elapsed,
That soon the sand
Began to vibrate, too,
Yet, still there was no sighting
And no clue,
When suddenly a movement sent Fox
Moving back a bit.
The ground was thumping violently,
The marching course and thick,
And as he watched

*JaniceT*

It coming o'er the rise
He saw them, glowing red,
A thousand eyes.
The marching, armied scorpions
With poison pointed tails
Came nearer, then abruptly stopped,
And all to silence fell.
In this arena, blue and white
And cold,
The desert felt victoriously
Bold.


For several hours neither faction
Made but subtle moves,
And all the while little Fox
Was planning whet he'd do
To somehow circumvent
The enemy.
A plan arose and slowly then
Did he.
When first Fox moved a little right
And then a little left,
In either case the scorpions
Would mirror what he did.
Their tiny legs in strict,
Unyielding sets
Showed Fox the limitations
Of their steps.
He'd studied well this battleground
While they were facing off.
He thought the sand beyond the dune
Might very well be soft;
The scorpions had churned it,
Leaving scars.


*Echoes*

It's distance seemed
The only ill so far.
In slow retreat Fox took his aim.
The scorpions approached,
And though he did increase his step,
They kept their body slowed.
Fox watched the distance
'Tween him and his foe
Upon this high, hard dune
Of whiteness grow.
Just as their tiny footsteps doubled
Fox's way was clear.
With every pound of strength he bounded
Forward; death stood near.
Then, suddenly, Fox leapt
Into the sky
And arched across the air
Light as a sigh.
He flapped and giggled, fox-like bird,
On o'er the scorpions.
But then the sand came rushing up
As if to swallow him.
He fell and rolled and tumbled
O'er the ground.
The sand was not so very soft,
He found.

The moon and stars looked down upon
An angry desert floor
Where little Fox was stumbling to
His feet, quite dazed and sore.
The desert ordered scorpions
To chase
This tired Fox,

*JaniceT*

But 'twas a sorry race
For Fox's heart was glued to going
Home, despite his fall.
Now, unconcerned with scorpions,
He soon outran them all.
The desert tried to
Usher up a wind
To hold Fox back,
But breezes did it vend.
On these transparent waves was born
An odor sweet though thin
Whose tresses teased young Fox's nostrils
Tantalizing him.
The scent spun flowers, trees,
And moist, cool earth
Through Fox's mind,
But caution had he learned.
With mild approval Fox took on
This vaporous hand as guide,
Though now and then he'd look to see
Which way the stars did glide.
The glowing gown on high
And wafting breeze
Were synchronizing course;
Fox was relieved.
The desert, as it's rage grew more
Intense, evoked less harm,
Entangled as an octopus
With eight great knotted arms,
And could not cause the breeze
To cease nor blow,
Nor counter the direction
Fox would go.
The rotating midnight silver

*Echoes*

Moon began to wane.
Fox knew that 'fore too long the
Penetrating dark would reign.
And though the stars would
Draw upon the sky,
To pits and perils
Fox might soon be blind.

An aching and exhausted Fox
Trod o'er the warming sand.
Again his eyes were burning
With day's light upon the land.
His empty belly churned
And begged relief,
But odors on the air
Did spare his grief.
The total scene was sizzling
When vaguely Fox perceived
That straight ahead a blur was dancing;
Dancing to deceive?
He closed his eyes
To follow just his nose
And as he did the
Vapors rose and rose.
The scent grew to a thick perfume,
Then to a lush, dense fog.
Fox hesitantly pried one eye
To opening and saw
His forest home
A little ways away
His heart began to bloom
And body quake.
Fox dredged his every energy
From deep within the bone,

*JaniceT*

Then, in a burst of several strides,
He brought his body home.
As tree-born shade
Enveloped him anew
He slowed, then dropped
Beside an old, clear pool.
Fox lapped the water lazily
And breathed a tired sigh.
Reflections spoke of leery friends
And family nearby.
When dripping muzzle lifted
On this cue
Their missing Fox was
Home again they knew.
As cheers rang up and all drew near
Fox told to them his tale.
Not far away the desert lay
Still snarled and rage-impelled.
It hadn't learned,
It hadn't learned a tid,
But then, of course,
The desert never did.

JaniceT

# Shanty Town

The sun goes down on Shanty Town
And drags all light away
And not one moonbeam touches ground
Though numerous are they.
Not even do the eyes of owls
Pervade the ebon night
Where air is foul, where stray dogs howl,
And babes cry through the night.

# My Heart Upon A Loom

My heart upon a loom,
Each woven cord revealing
An incidence of you;
It's you who do the weaving.
Though guarded I this heart
'Neath coolest countenance
You took a gentler part
Than I could guard against.

My heart upon a loom
Which many years lay barren
And I seemed long unmoved;
Thus, uncompleted therein.
You took a crimson strand
Against my warning eye.
With patient, agile hand
You wove away the lie.

My heart upon a loom.
Now row by row a passion
By which I am consumed
Within this frame is fashioned.
A woolen cloak we weave
To keep us from such cold
As loneliness can breed
When maids and men grow old.

# Skyline

There is a pattern upon the land
Following no pattern at all.
Rubies, diamonds, emeralds and jade
Adorn every rhythm of man,
Showing a canopy of stars as pale
Above their silent brilliance.
Though clouds and fog may briefly
Obscure the witnessing of heavenly stars,
"Tis a vapor of many forms
Could put an end
To the lights of man.

JaniceT

# Drowned Ship of Prey

The ship went down one stormy winter's eve
And not one man survived to render why
But on the harbor bottom lay her wreck
Where anchored nets reach up for open sky.

Lashed to the mast her captain's bones remain
As fishermen became the food of fish
Which play amongst the tatters of her sails
And tour the sunken vessel as they wish.

Now through the broken body of her hull
All manner of aquatic creatures roam,
Although intended as a ship of prey
Her prey have found, within her bosom, home.

# The Train

His constant focus lies beyond the glass,
Beyond the changing vistas gliding past
To that one point, his final destination
Where he will disembark this train at last.

He wears a smile, a camouflage expression,
A mask to hide impatience and depression.
Dark disappointment holds him, nails him down
But of this he gives no one an impression.

I watch him from the far side of the coach.
As other passengers make their approach
His tight, white fists spring open, greeting each
And clutch fast, as they leave, as if reproached.

From time to time he finds himself invited
To other coaches, and he seems delighted,
But always does he give some mild excuse,
No matter how the other appears slighted,

Because his whole attention tends to grasp
Beyond the changing vistas gliding past
To that one point, his final destination
Where he will disembark this train at last.

# Such In The Nature Of Love

Even the hardiest seed will spoil
Sewn into infertile, shallow soil
Placed in a cup on a window sill
Shoots getting hotter and hotter still
Ill tended, unwatered, and left to die;
Such in the nature of love was I.

Deep in the darkness of forest shade
Seldom a sapling can bear one blade
Starving for water, for light and food
These eked away by the neighborhood
Where desperate dealings alone apply;
Such in the nature of love was I.

Forests axed open, a seed resewn;
Thus was I rescued by love alone
Watered and warmed with your slightest touch
Ever my aim to return as much
And more to this vessel in which we lie;
Such in the nature of love am I.

# Neptune's Gift

Out across the waves, from untold fathoms,
A swath of sea gave up to boiling foam
Erupting ever wide in high flung fountain
He rose, ass-high, colossus, mammoth, bold
And rage was in his face of twisted flesh
Bronze, tortured muscle gripping something old
Of pipes and keyboard, gold and coral meshed.
And from his deepest agony he moaned
Then briefly gazed aground in his torment
While each contracting fiber gave to throw
And mightily hurl long the instrument.
Out toward the rolling hills and bay-side shoals
It vaulted through the air, like Thor's great hammer,
Came crashing, splintered, sprawled, cacophony
Which slowly settled down to echoed clamor
While Neptune glided back into the sea.
A coastal folk, who witnessed his endeavor,
Made sport of Neptune's folly, seemingly,
Then set about up-righting pipes and keyboard
And of the rubble build huge factories.
Now, through the haze of centuries is visioned
Before polluted eyes the present sight
Of chimneys belching fumes devoid of rhythm
In unrelenting discord day and night
While passing ships and buoys on the ocean
Spend 'ore the beach their disconnected tones,
And, I can't help but ponder on a notion:
What ever happened to the coral and gold?

*Echoes*

# Endless Orchards

A two lane ribbon of road
Stretched tight across the valley floor
Bisecting deep and low
The endless orchards, now of yore.

Against the distant hills,
Soft sentries, washed with Summer's gold,
The verdant green did swell
As if to reach beyond their hold.

So often did I cruise
Beneath enormous azure skies
Along that beauteous route
Before the endless orchards died.

# Mr. Bleak's Tomatoes

The land was thin, exhausted, bled,
Where Mr. Bleak's tomatoes fed
On substances contrived to force
A hastening of Nature's course.
Globes of sunlight, pipe-fed shower
'Neath a vaulted plastic bower,
Lavished with a lethal spray
To keep all other life at bay.
Thus did Bleak's tomatoes grow,
Mile upon mile and row by row.

Weeks elapsed as branches bent,
Pulled by the fruit which clung to them
'Till, plump and round and lush, yet green,
Mr. Bleak began to glean
As many plants as met in size
The uniform of his device,
Replanting each on open ground
He covered them with new compounds
And toxic fumes that filled the air.
Even the birds will not fly there.

The noxious compost in their bed
Coerces them from green to red,
Then off to market will they go
To lie in orchestrated rows
Disguised as produce fit to eat
For each has perfect, ripe-red meat.
And Mr. Bleak begins anew
With tender seed and volatile brew.
Thus do Bleak's tomatoes grow,
Mile upon mile and row by row.

*Echoes*

# Heartscapes

Within my heart lies country
That I had called my own,
Until I gained that you'd obtained
A foothold in this zone.

At first it seemed unlikely,
But then I came to see,
With hesitance, the residence
You'd taken up in me

In time I came to trust you,
To let your presence grow,
As did my own affection for
The man I've come to know.

Now, when I'm lost I feel you,
My compass, map, and star,
For you are ever present in
The landscape of my heart.

*Echoes*

# When None Command

By surging sea and force of wind
A tattered vessel floundered in
Where coral reef performed the rest
In ripping wide her wooden breast.
From timber scream to cracking mast
Her form dismembered to the last
And on the waves her pieces reached
An aftermath of slumber, beached.
She is a silent reprimand
To those who sail
When none command.

# Epitaph

Engraven granite legacy placed
'Ore a dead man's tomb of earth;
His life was leaving this alone behind
In signature of worth
And Potters Field abounds with vacant
Stone above our common dead
Where Mozart's body found it's last repose.
I'd rather this instead
Of life in dormant atmospheres and
Owing to another hand
To chisel out my immortality'
To mark a plot of land.
Thus, owing to my work in art through
Verse, should I leave life, unknown,
At least I will have tried to lend my worth
Beyond the token stone.

## How Deep Are The Oceans

How deep are the oceans of this maiden's heart?
How many treasured secrets can it hold
Or sorrows bear and there to burst apart
Upon the jagged stones of thwarted goals?

Though all events in life may prove to be
A means of taking soundings, this I know
There is a greater reason to proceed:
In each adventure my heart tells me so.

*Janice T*

~~ Thank you ~~

If you are interested in finding more information
about the poetry of JaniceT, visit her blog at:
janice-t.weebly.com

60403441R00040

Made in the USA
Charleston, SC
31 August 2016